MW01079542

POETRY
OF THE HEART
AND MIND

C.C. MATTHEWS

Fulton Books, Inc.
Meadville, PA

Published by Fulton Books 2021

ISBN 978-1-63710-092-9 (hardcover)
ISBN 978-1-63710-091-2 (digital)

Printed in the United States of America

This book of poems is dedicated to a wonderful woman who passed away on December 1, 2009. We were not only close friends, but we also had a relationship that is so extremely hard to find that many people strive to find in a lifetime. She meant the world to me and I to her. When we were away from one another, we fall asleep while on the phone with each other. When we were together, those moments of silence most people feel awkward about were okay to us. We were perfectly content with each other's company. We talked about marriage and family but couldn't reach that point due to life's unexpected twists.

People have asked me how I continue to get up in the morning. My answer is simple. She was the type of person who would find a way to kick my behind if I didn't continue living my life being the man who always looks on the positive side, the man who always chooses to see and believe there is still good in people, and the man she fell in love with. She said she understood why it never worked out with anyone else and couldn't wait to spend the rest of her life with me. Even though we weren't married, she was, without a doubt, my wife. You're in my heart forever.

In loving memory of Hannah (July 20, 1988–December 1, 2009).

DAYS

Day after day, night after night
I dream of you so that we might
Have that chance to be together
To fall in love forever and ever

And now you're gone to a place unknown
It feels as if you're there alone
It's hard enough knowing you're gone
But our love will remain
Forever strong

Each growing day
Since you've been gone
I can't believe I'm still this strong
Soul to soul, heart to heart
The love for you will never grow apart

The road I took has reached its end
So now I must begin again
The path I choose will never be wrong as
Long as you lead me along

Every day must come to an end
But every morning will begin again
The love and joy we had together
Will remain in my heart and thought
Forever and ever

DREAMS OF THE FUTURE

Dream a dream yet
Left open
Heal our wounds
Ripped wide open
A life together we
Dreamed someday
The love we had
Will always' s stay

I know in my heart
You're in a better place
But every morning
I'll see your face
The pain of love
I feel each day
I'll remember you
And say I love you
In so many ways

I know someday
We'll be back together
And on that day
Up in the heavens
I'll be there on one
Knee proposing
As I promised
I would someday

SEARCHING AGAIN

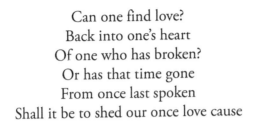

Can one find love?
Back into one's heart
Of one who has broken?
Or has that time gone
From once last spoken
Shall it be to shed our once love cause

Left wide open
To fight what's right
Left not spoken
Lead us to what's decided
But our heart's desires can't be
Discarded

To start a new
A life with you
Let's look forward
And yet to come
And leave behind
What can't be undone?

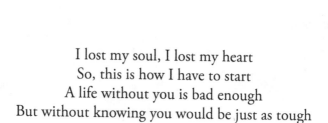

LOST

I lost my soul, I lost my heart
So, this is how I have to start
A life without you is bad enough
But without knowing you would be just as tough

Every night I dream of you
To make a wish that won't come true
The pain of love I feel each day
I look at the sky and say
I'll be on my way

Even though the poem is
Dark and blue
I'll be happy just for you
The road ahead will be long
But I promise I'll remain strong

My deepest fear may have come true
I'll be completely alone without you
Knowing this is hard to bear
I just keep thinking this is unfair

It's hard to change how I feel
When I lost something so real
You were my life
My heart, my soul
Baby, I love you so here I go

INNOCENCE'S

The ocean breezes
the sky full of the sun's rays
there you are clear as day
and when you're down the sky's turns gray
but I know you know
tomorrows a new day
you're smart and gorgeous
and full of life
don't waste another moment in your past
your future is here
but now you can't tell
just years from now you'll be saying wow!

FIVE YEARS

Five years, sixty months
One thousand eight hundred twenty-five days
Forty-three thousand eight hundred hours
Two million six hundred twenty right thousand seconds

Times are good, and times are bad
We try to live, the life's we have
It's hard and short and hard to bear
This world of ours is just unfair

We work and work
And rest each day
And yet we push
Many things away

We need to learn
A new way to live
Before each life
Learns not to live

We need to love
And play sometime each day because
Our lives are at risk
Each day

TRUE LOVE

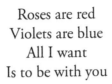

Roses are red
Violets are blue
All I want
Is to be with you

Every day from
Dawn to dusk
I think of you
And then I blush
And when it's time

To be together
We'll fall in love and live together
Until that day will have to
Trust our love for us
Is more than lust?

In that time then we will see
Our love for us will be you and me
And if it be you and me
Our love will be for eternity

FINDING MEANING

The meaning of love
Is hard to find
Savoring the thoughts
Of what we may find
The meaning of love
Can be blind

Time to time
Some will find
Their meaning of love
Some just can't find
The time we had
Can't be forgotten

But the pain of loss
Will always be haunting
Cause love and time
Can be hard to bear
Cause time itself
Just will not share

The time to love
The ones we care
It's hard to see
What love can be?
But I knew
You loved me

THE ONE

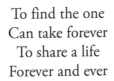

To find the one
Can take forever
To share a life
Forever and ever

I found the one
I loved and cared
We though our time
Would be spared

I lost my love
With no time to spare
In my heart I knew
This was not fair
Cause time had played
That deadly stare

In that time
Our life a new
We knew in our hearts
Our love was true

To search again
I will not find
That true love
We had just in time

LIFE

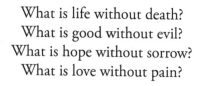

What is life without death?
What is good without evil?
What is hope without sorrow?
What is love without pain?

Do they hold meaning?
To what we call life
Or do they just define
Our twisted way of life

If we consider that life is just
Then does life hold purpose
How can one know?
When society itself
Is full of the unknown

To consider such thinking
Some would say to be not all there
But to this I hold to be unfair

To one who thinks of this?
We shall have to bear
It's logic and reasoning that brings us there

THE TRUTH

I want to know the answers to why
It's hard to shut the door
And leave behind so many questions
Float in my mind

I'm a man of action
But completely lost within
The reactions of life, you can't seem to win

Why can't we be the ones
That have control, pulling the strings that lead below
I don't care what you plan, I want mine!

As time goes by, we can lose or way
From which our Forefathers gave
The fight is not with others, it's with our selves

I have nothing left to give
Disappear into the dirt
Light the way and ill end where I began

The truth will drag you down till the end
Life is full of questions and wonder
Facing a faceless enemy
That everyone knows by looking in the mirror

BRIGHTNESS

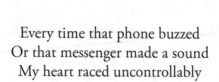

Every time that phone buzzed
Or that messenger made a sound
My heart raced uncontrollably

Talking to you always made the bad day
Seem not bad at all, just knowing
That you were mine for the taking
Kept my heart racing

The day we first talked
I knew right then and there
You were the one I need
To complete my life

So when that day comes
When we're up at the alter
Watching you walk up to me
Knowing I'll be right next to
Every night and morning
To see your Beautiful face

It is and has been a dream come true

EXPRESSING

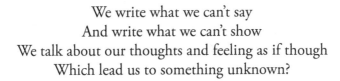

We write what we can't say
And write what we can't show
We talk about our thoughts and feeling as if though
Which lead us to something unknown?

The feeling I had about being alone
Has changed by your words alone
I'm scared and nervous
From what happened to me before

But I think with you
The fears will go free
Your love, your care
May bring me back from once before

The words we exchange
From our hearts and minds
Bring us together
From worlds beyond

THE CALL

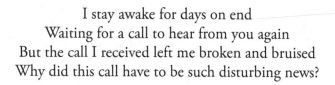

I stay awake for days on end
Waiting for a call to hear from you again
But the call I received left me broken and bruised
Why did this call have to be such disturbing news?

Heavy breathing to weightless feeling
Thoughts to memories rip the ceiling
How can my world be so deceiving?
My dreams my hopes come crashing down
Pushing me beneath the ground

Lying here upon the floor
Drowning in tears my body pours
With no feeling though out my body
Will I survive and escape this hole
That my world has brought upon my soul

In this state, there is no sound
I yell and scream, but no one's around
I used what strength I had to get up
Out this hole, I travel the town with
Nowhere to go

Walking for hours with nothing to show
Lost in circles-in the bitter cold
Listening for the sound that's not around

At the end of my walk
I found myself
Back where I started

WHAT'S THIS FEELING?

This feeling I get around you
Leads me to believe that
When I sing this song
We'll always have each other
When everything clse is gone

That constant heart beating motion
That butterfly sensational explosion
In every moment, of every emotion

What is this that I feel—is that passion?
Or is that lust
Or just maybe, maybe, it could be love

This feeling held so deep within
Oh, where do I begin?
To explain this feeling deep within

This feeling you give
Uncovers the better part of me
This turns me into another
And reminds me that we'll
Always have each other

No matter where we've gone

FREE SPIRIT

The way you dance
The way you move
Can light up any room
You dance with grace
As a flower bloom

As you dance upon a stage
You glance into the crowed
With that heartwarming gaze
To see me there, looking up at you

You knew that your dreams had come true
As I watch you dance upon the stage
I see just how much you gave
I'm glad to see you dream to be

Dancing and being just with me
At the end of a show
I know you would run into my arms

YEARS

So much time has passed from once I have heard you last
As I sit and think and glance through the past
I wish we had just one more laugh
Seven years have driven past
Not once have I forgotten the broken glass
That ripped through my heart
And left an open gash

You'll always be my number one
Through present and past
My future feels like an hourglass
The sands rush through
Like my feelings as I write about you
Your voice and beauty burned in my head
As your love and passion run deep in my heart
Our soul was one, but now it's gone
I fight each day to build what's gone
I find myself exactly where I belong

In a new city, in a new state, new friends
To change the pace even though
I'll always see your face
I know I belong in this place
To build a new faith not in God, not in grace
But in myself as I look at my face
Not sure what I'll find as I walk through time
But I know in my heart and mind
I'll be fine and things will work out in due time

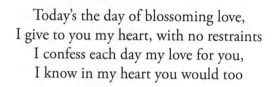

VALENTINE'S DAY

Today's the day of blossoming love,
I give to you my heart, with no restraints
I confess each day my love for you,
I know in my heart you would too

Life is too short, so break the rules
Forgive quickly, kiss slowly, love truly,
And most of all
Never regret anything that made you smile

When I looked into your eyes
I didn't see just you, I saw my today,
My tomorrow, and my future
Till the rest of my life

Flowers, chocolates, and cards
Are great too for such a day
But I wanted something to
Last more than a day
For you to look back on
To smile each day
As I look at you to say
I love you

YOU

Your smile, your heart, your thoughts
Are the greatest I've ever known
It makes me feel like we were one soul

On the day we first meet, our hearts were a fluster
Just the thoughts made me wonder
A life with you would be like no other
Like painting a picture and seeing what's discovered
Your presence and grace are gifts from above
You fill my heart with so much love

I've seen your charm, your beauty
The unfathomable grace in your face
As I close my eyes to erase, to start anew
My heart will be bound with passion
To write, to teach, to search

For that love we had shared
To connect again, with no regrets of the truth
A shadow of light will put to rest
With a new slate of certainty
To cross out of what I have done
To who I have become

NOW

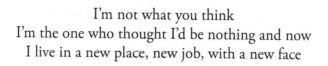

I'm not what you think
I'm the one who thought I'd be nothing and now
I live in a new place, new job, with a new face

In this place needing to feel alive
I write like I'm no alive
To tell a tale of once upon a time
My fears have come alive

You knew my heart, you knew my face
I have lost sight, so don't count on me
As the sun chases me

I've cut the strings that held me still
And broke through my irony
Searching a new, road to walk and run
Where did I think I could go?

FAMILY

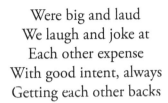

Were big and laud
We laugh and joke at
Each other expense
With good intent, always
Getting each other backs

Nothing will change what's become
Just the people who inspired
Us to do our best

We may have never met each other's families
But I know they would have fit
Like a puzzle piece

NEW

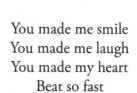

You made me smile
You made me laugh
You made my heart
Beat so fast

We both said "I love you"
We felt it would last
You broke my heart
Like in my past

You erased every moment
Like nothing past
Did I even matter
I guess I was just a big laugh

No friends no family
Is now what I have
I start again from my past
I've learned a lesson

Love is a word which now holds no meaning
I'll live my life with no more feeling
I num myself to feel no pain
Because life itself is a bullshit game

You can say I'm a lost man
In a lost world
The values I hold true
Have withered and died
I am now completely
Nothing inside

I'm not lost, I haven't miss spoken
My morals and values
Are no longer sought out
For this world, we now live
From here on out

END

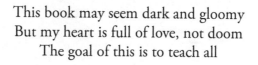

This book may seem dark and gloomy
But my heart is full of love, not doom
The goal of this is to teach all

That life is life, it may or may not have an end
Stop and breathe and move again
Don't dwell on past things, just remember the moments
Of joy and happiness

It's okay to feel such pain and misery
The key is to gain open visibility
Learn to cope, find your peace

Create an outlet for you to reach
I may seem sad, I may seem broken
But my heart is pure, and my eyes are open

Everyone is different, and each situation
But one commonality is help is always open
I found my help in the form of writing

I'm not looking for fame or fortune
Simply share human emotions
We are social in nature, looking for a bond

The lesson to take from this
Is that life is a journey
Don't let it beat you down, or you'll miss all the beauty

About the Author

Born and raised in a small town in upstate New York, C. C. Matthews always knew he wanted to make an impact on the world even at a young age. After traveling across the United States and gathering inspiration from the different communities and cultures that make each area so unique, C. C. Matthews finally learned what his true calling was in life. C. C. discovered that he had an innate ability to express and share his experiences, passion, and wisdom with the rest of the world through literature, making each day a bit brighter one poem or story at a time.

C. C. takes his audience on a journey with each narrative as he cascades through the adventures as only he knows how with the hopes to inspire and touch each and every soul that joins them along the way. C. C.'s favorite quote is "Some men see things as they are and ask why. I dream of things that never were and ask why not" by Robert F. Kennedy

C. C. feels that if helping one person is considered a random act of kindness, then helping millions is a goal yet to be accomplished.

CPSIA information can be obtained
at www.ICGtesting.com
Printed in the USA
BVHW031739040621
608822BV00011B/2764/J